ADHD Cleaning and Organizing Hacks

Practical Strategies for Keeping Your Home while thriving with ADHD

Matthew Haller

Copyright © 2024 by Matthew Haller

All rights reserved.

No portion of this book may be reproduced in any form without written permission from the publisher or author, except as permitted by U.S. copyright law.

Table of Contents

Introduction

Understanding Your ADHD Brain and Why Cleaning Feels Hard

The Benefits of Creating Organized Systems

How This Book Can Help You Take Control

Chapter 1: Out with the Old: Decluttering Strategies that Work for ADHD

The "Spark Joy" Method - Not Quite There for ADHD?

The Batching Method: Conquer the Clutter in Bursts

The Decision Wheel: Overcome Analysis Paralysis

The Emotional Clutter: Letting Go of Sentimental Items

Chapter 2: Containment Chaos: Creating Storage Solutions that Stick

Identifying Storage Needs Based on Your ADHD Tendencies

Labeling Everything (Seriously, Everything!)

Utilizing Clear Containers and Organizers

Multifunctional Furniture: Saving Space and Sanity

Chapter 3: Paper Tsunami: Taming the Paperwork Monster

Going Digital: Embracing Paperless Systems

The Quick-Sort Method: Dealing with Incoming Paperwork

Creating Designated Drop Zones for Paperwork

Filing Systems that Don't Fail You (and Your Attention Span)

Chapter 4: Breaking Down the Walls: Chunking Tasks for ADHD Brains

The Pomodoro Technique: Cleaning in Focused Sprints

The "Blitz Cleaning" Method: Quick Bursts of Activity

Creating Visual Task Lists with Checkboxes

Rewarding Yourself: Making Cleaning Fun (or at Least Tolerable)

Chapter 5: Conquering Cleaning Consistency: Building Habits that Last

The Power of Routines: Creating a Cleaning Schedule that Sticks

Habit Stacking: Attach Cleaning to Existing Routines

Taming the Perfectionist: Focusing on Progress, Not Perfection

Enlisting Help (Without Feeling Like a Failure)

Chapter 6: Technology to the Rescue: Apps and Gadgets for ADHD Cleaning

Utilizing Cleaning Timers and Apps

Smart Home Devices to Automate Tasks (Yes, Really!)

Noise-Canceling Headphones: Tuning Out Distractions While You Clean

Investing in Cleaning Tools That Make Life Easier

Chapter 7: The One-Minute Tidy: Quick Pick-Me-Ups to Prevent Overwhelm

The "Put-Away Patrol": Training Yourself to Return Items Immediately

The Evening Reset: A Quick Tidy Before Bed

The Weekend Warrior: Scheduling Deeper Cleaning Sessions

Chapter 8: Embracing Imperfections: Self-Compassion for the ADHD Cleaner

Letting Go of the "Shoulds": Creating Realistic

Expectations

Forgive Yourself for Setbacks: Progress, Not Perfection

Celebrating Your Achievements: Building Confidence and Motivation

Chapter 9: Long-Term Strategies: Preventing Relapse and Maintaining Order

Identifying Triggers for Clutter: Understanding Your ADHD Patterns

Re-evaluating Regularly: Adapting Systems as Your Needs Change

Creating a Support System: Enlisting Help When Needed

Conclusion: Living with ADHD: Creating Calm and Order in a Chaotic World

The shrill beeping of the smoke alarm was the rude awakening I didn't need. Except, it wasn't the smoke alarm. It was my toaster, valiantly trying to signal its fiery demise through a thick curtain of burnt toast smoke. My heart hammered a frantic rhythm against my ribs as I fumbled for the fire extinguisher, dodging a precariously balanced mountain of clothes threatening to topple from the ironing board like an avalanche.

This was just another Tuesday in the whirlwind that was my life. My name is Maya, and I have ADHD, which translates to a constant symphony of chaos playing in my head. It's like living in a house where all the appliances are set to "high," the lights flicker erratically, and the furniture rearranges itself at night.

Finding my keys was the first skirmish of the day. I vaguely remembered shoving them into a "bowl" somewhere, but my definition of "bowl" apparently encompassed every flat surface in the apartment. After a frantic ten-minute search, I unearthed them from under a pile of mail that rivaled Mount Everest in height. By the time I wrestled the keys from the papery clutches, the smoke alarm/toaster debacle had unfolded, adding a layer of acrid urgency to my already frazzled state.

The laundry situation was another testament to the war I waged daily against entropy. Clothes sprouted from every corner like rogue vines, defying the laws of gravity and organization. Ironing, a task I loathed with the passion of a thousand suns, usually ended up being a last-minute battle against wrinkles, resulting in the current teetering tower threatening to engulf me in a landslide of cotton and polyester.

This wasn't how I envisioned adulting. I dreamt of a serene apartment, not a chaotic obstacle course. A place where the only drama came from a good book, not a runaway toaster or a rebellious sock that refused to pair with its mate. But with ADHD, even the simplest tasks morphed into epic struggles.

The burnt toast incident, however, proved to be a turning point. As I surveyed the damage, a strange calm settled over me. Maybe, just maybe, there was a better way. A way to tame the chaos, to create a system that worked for my ADHD brain. This book is the chronicle of that journey, a battle plan for fellow warriors fighting against the clutter and disorganization that comes with ADHD. It's a promise that with the right strategies and a healthy dose of self-compassion, we can build an oasis of calm in the midst of the whirlwind.

Understanding Your ADHD Brain and Why Cleaning Feels Hard

The burnt toast incident wasn't just about a malfunctioning appliance; it was a metaphor for the constant struggle many of us with ADHD face. Our brains are wired differently. They're like powerful race cars with a steering wheel that sometimes spins wildly out of control.

Executive function, the brain's control center for planning, organization, and focus, is often compromised in ADHD. This can make tasks like cleaning feel overwhelming. Here's why:

Trouble with Initiation: Getting started can be the biggest hurdle. We might get stuck in analysis paralysis, overwhelmed by the sheer volume of the mess.

Focus and Attention: Shiny objects (or squirrels, in the metaphorical sense) abound, easily distracting us from the cleaning at hand.

Time Management: Our perception of time can be skewed, leading to underestimation of how long a task will take, resulting in missed deadlines (or burnt toast).

Working Memory: Holding onto instructions and multi-tasking can be a challenge. We might forget what cleaning supplies we need, or get sidetracked halfway through a task.

These challenges don't make us lazy or incapable. They simply mean we need to approach cleaning differently.

The Benefits of Creating Organized Systems

Imagine a world where your keys have a designated spot, your laundry magically folds itself, and the dishes wash themselves (okay, maybe not that last one, but a girl can dream!). Creating organized systems is the key to unlocking a calmer, more manageable life with ADHD. Here's how:

Reduces Decision Fatigue: Clear routines and designated spots eliminate the constant need to decide what to do next, freeing up mental energy for other things.

Minimizes Distractions: A clutter-free environment reduces visual distractions, allowing you to focus on the cleaning task at hand.

Improves Time Management: Breaking down cleaning into smaller, manageable chunks helps you stay on track and avoid feeling overwhelmed.

Boosts Self-Esteem: A clean and organized environment can be incredibly empowering, fostering a sense of accomplishment and control over your surroundings.

How This Book Can Help You Take Control

This book is your personal battle plan for conquering the chaos of cleaning with ADHD. We'll explore strategies tailored to the way your brain works, offering practical tips and tricks to:

Declutter like a pro: Learn effective strategies to tame the clutter and create functional storage solutions.

Break down cleaning into manageable chunks: Discover techniques like the Pomodoro Technique to tackle cleaning in focused sprints.

Build cleaning routines that stick: Explore habit stacking and other methods to create cleaning schedules that work for you.

Embrace technology as your cleaning ally: Learn how apps, timers, and smart home devices can become your secret weapons.

Develop self-compassion: We'll talk about letting go of perfectionism and celebrating your progress, no matter how small.

Remember, creating a calm and organized space is a journey, not a destination. There will be setbacks, there will be burnt toast incidents. But with the right tools and a supportive community (that's you and this book!), you can transform your cleaning routine from a battlefield to a manageable, even (dare we say?) enjoyable experience. So, grab your metaphorical fire extinguisher, let's ditch the burnt toast, and embark on this journey together!

Chapter 1: Out with the Old: Decluttering Strategies that Work for ADHD

The battle against clutter is often the first line of defense in creating an organized space. But for those of us with ADHD, staring down a mountain of possessions can feel paralyzing. Don't worry, fellow warriors! This chapter will equip you with decluttering strategies specifically designed to work with your ADHD brain.

The "Spark Joy" Method - Not Quite There for ADHD?

You've probably heard of the KonMari method, where you hold each item and ask yourself if it "sparks joy." While this approach can be helpful, it doesn't always resonate with the ADHD brain. Here's why:

Decision Fatigue: Constantly evaluating every single item can be mentally draining.

Emotional Attachment: We might hold onto things for sentimental reasons, even if they don't bring us joy in the present moment.

Don't despair! We have alternative approaches that are more ADHD-friendly.

The Batching Method: Conquer the Clutter in Bursts

Our brains thrive on short bursts of focused activity. Here's how to use batching to your advantage:

1. Set a Timer: Choose a time limit (20 minutes is a good starting point) and commit to decluttering for that duration.

2. Target a Specific Area: Focus on one drawer, shelf, or category of items (clothes, books, etc.) at a time.

3. Sort ruthlessly: Ask yourself these questions:
Have I used this in the past year?
Does it still serve a purpose?
Would I buy this again if I saw it in a store?

Tip: Play some upbeat music while you declutter. It can help you stay focused and motivated.

The Decision Wheel: Overcome Analysis Paralysis

Sometimes, the sheer volume of decisions can lead to overwhelm. Here's a tool to help you make quick choices:

1. Create a Decision Wheel: Divide a piece of paper into sections labeled "Keep," "Donate," "Trash," and "Maybe."

2. Spin the Wheel (Optional): For items you're truly undecided about, give fate a little nudge by spinning the wheel.
3. Trust the Process: Even if the wheel lands on "Maybe," revisit the item later with a fresher perspective.

Tip: Use brightly colored sections on your wheel to make it visually engaging.

The Emotional Clutter: Letting Go of Sentimental Items

Letting go of sentimental items can be especially challenging. Here are some strategies to help:

Take Photos: Capture the memory with a picture before letting go of the physical object.
Create a Memory Box: Curate a collection of items that represent a significant portion of your life.

Write a Letter: Express your gratitude for the item and the memories it holds before saying goodbye.

Remember, letting go doesn't erase the memory. It simply creates space for new experiences.

By using these strategies, you can transform the decluttering process from a daunting chore into a series of manageable tasks.

Chapter 2: Containment Chaos: Creating Storage Solutions that Stick

You've bravely tackled the clutter mountain, and now it's time to create a system that keeps it at bay. But with ADHD, traditional storage solutions can sometimes become their own source of chaos. Fear not, warriors! This chapter will equip you with strategies to design storage that works for your unique brain.

Identifying Storage Needs Based on Your ADHD Tendencies

The first step is understanding your own tendencies. Here are some common ADHD traits and their storage solutions:

Out of sight, out of mind: If you tend to forget things easily, prioritize open storage or clear containers.

Impulse buyer: Create designated "catch-all" zones to prevent clutter from spreading.

Easily distracted: Minimize visual clutter by using closed storage for less frequently used items.

By understanding your tendencies, you can create a storage system that complements your brain, not battles it.

Labeling Everything (Seriously, Everything!)

Our brains crave clarity. Labeling everything, from drawers to shelves to containers, can be a game-changer. Here's why:

Reduced Decision Fatigue: Clear labels eliminate the need to rummage and guess what's inside.

Improved Organization: Labeled storage makes it easier to put things back in their designated spot.

Visual Cues: Labels serve as visual reminders, helping you remember where things are located.

Tip: Use colorful labels, pictures, or even emojis to make them visually engaging and fun.

Utilizing Clear Containers and Organizers

Out-of-sight, out-of-mind doesn't have to mean out-of-reach. Clear containers allow you to see what's inside, while keeping dust and clutter at bay. Here are some tips:

Categorize by Use: Group similar items together within containers (e.g., all socks in one container, workout clothes in another).

Dividers are Your Friend: Use dividers within drawers or containers to further categorize items.

Transparent Shelves: Consider replacing opaque shelves with clear ones for better visibility.

Tip: Invest in stackable containers to maximize space and create a cohesive look.

Multifunctional Furniture: Saving Space and Sanity

Small apartments often mean limited storage space. Multifunctional furniture can be your secret weapon. Here are some ideas:

Ottomans with Storage: Store blankets, throw pillows, or even board games inside an ottoman.

Beds with Drawers: Utilize the space underneath your bed for clothes, shoes, or seasonal items.

Baskets and Bins: Stylish baskets can double as storage for toys, magazines, or throws.

Tip: Choose furniture with clean lines and a neutral color palette to create a sense of calm in your space.

By implementing these strategies, you can transform your storage from a chaotic black hole to a system that supports your ADHD brain. The next chapter will tackle the paper monster – the bane of many an ADHD warrior's existence!

Chapter 3: Paper Tsunami: Taming the Paperwork Monster

The ever-growing pile of bills, receipts, and random notes – the paper tsunami – is a common foe for those with ADHD. But fear not, warriors! This chapter will equip you with strategies to navigate the paperwork deluge and establish a system that keeps it under control.

Going Digital: Embracing Paperless Systems

In today's digital age, there's a solution for almost everything – including paper clutter! Here are some ways to go paperless:

E-Statements and Bills: Opt for electronic statements and bills from your bank, credit card companies, and service providers.

Online Bill Pay: Set up automatic bill payments to avoid late fees and paper clutter.

Digital Receipts: Many stores offer digital receipts emailed to your inbox, eliminating the need for paper ones.

Scanning Important Documents: Scan important documents like warranties or contracts and store them securely in a cloud storage app.

Going paperless not only declutters your physical space but also makes it easier to find documents later.

The Quick-Sort Method: Dealing with Incoming Paperwork

Even in a digital age, some paper will inevitably find its way into your home. Here's a strategy to deal with it efficiently:

1. Designated Drop Zone: Create a specific location, like a tray or basket, for incoming mail and paperwork.

2. Daily Quick Sort: Dedicate a few minutes each day to sort through the drop zone.

3. Action Stations: Have designated areas for items that need action (to be paid, filed, etc.) and those that can be recycled immediately.

Tip: Set a timer for 5-10 minutes to keep the sorting session focused and manageable.

Creating Designated Drop Zones for Paperwork

Out of sight, out of mind doesn't work for most of us with ADHD. Here's how designated drop zones can help:

Multiple Drop Zones: Consider having separate drop zones for different types of paper (e.g., mail, bills, schoolwork).

Visually Appealing Zones: Use colorful trays or baskets to make the drop zones visually appealing, encouraging you to use them.

Empty Regularly: Schedule a time each week to empty the drop zones and take action on the accumulated paperwork.

Tip: Place the drop zones in high-traffic areas like your entryway or kitchen counter to serve as a constant reminder.

Filing Systems that Don't Fail You (and Your Attention Span)

Filing cabinets can be a graveyard for good intentions. Here's how to create a filing system that works with your ADHD brain:

Simple is Key: Use broad categories for filing instead of overly detailed ones.

Limit the Number of Files: Having too many files can be overwhelming. Start with a few main categories and adjust as needed.

Digital Filing Systems: Consider using digital filing systems for frequently accessed documents or those you don't need physical copies of.

Tip: Label your files clearly and consistently for easy retrieval. Use large fonts and bright colors to make them stand out.

By implementing these strategies, you can transform the paper tsunami into a manageable trickle. The next chapter will delve into creating cleaning routines that stick with your ADHD brain!

Chapter 4: Breaking Down the Walls: Chunking Tasks for ADHD Brains

The mere thought of cleaning an entire apartment can feel daunting for anyone, but for those of us with ADHD, it can be downright paralyzing. This chapter will equip you with strategies to break down cleaning tasks into manageable chunks, making the process less overwhelming and more achievable.

The Pomodoro Technique: Cleaning in Focused Sprints

Our brains thrive on short bursts of focused activity. The Pomodoro Technique, named after the tomato-shaped kitchen timer used by its inventor, is a perfect tool for this. Here's how to use it:

1. Set the Timer: Choose a time interval (25 minutes is a good starting point) and commit to cleaning during that period.
2. Focus on One Task: Pick a specific cleaning task (e.g., cleaning the bathroom mirror) and focus solely on that during the timer session.
3. Take a Short Break: When the timer rings, reward yourself with a short break (5 minutes is recommended).

Tip: During your break, step away from the cleaning zone entirely. Do some stretches, grab a snack, or check your phone (just set a timer to avoid getting sucked in!).

The Pomodoro Technique helps you stay focused, prevents mental fatigue, and provides a clear endpoint to the cleaning task.

The "Blitz Cleaning" Method: Quick Bursts of Activity

Sometimes, even 25 minutes feels like an eternity. The "Blitz Cleaning" method is perfect for those times when you need a quick burst of cleaning energy. Here's how it works:

1. Set a Timer for 5-10 Minutes: Choose a short timeframe and commit to cleaning as much as you can in that period.
2. Go All Out: Focus on a single area or task and clean with reckless abandon (within reason, of course!).
3. Stop When the Timer Rings: Even if you feel like continuing, stick to the timer to avoid burnout.

Tip: Put on some upbeat music and channel your inner cleaning warrior during the blitz session.

The "Blitz Cleaning" method is a great way to make a dent in a messy space without feeling overwhelmed.

Creating Visual Task Lists with Checkboxes

Our brains respond well to visual cues. Creating a visual task list with checkboxes can help you stay on track and motivated. Here's how:

1. Break Down Tasks into Smaller Steps: Instead of listing "Clean Kitchen," break it down into smaller, more manageable tasks like "Wipe down counters," "Empty dishwasher," and "Sweep floor."
2. Use Checkboxes: As you complete each step, check the corresponding box. Seeing completed tasks can be incredibly motivating.
3. Get Creative: Use colorful pens, stickers, or even drawings to make your task list visually engaging.

Tip: Consider using a whiteboard or a large piece of paper that you can hang in a central location to serve as a constant reminder.

Rewarding Yourself: Making Cleaning Fun (or at Least Tolerable)

Positive reinforcement goes a long way with ADHD brains. Rewarding yourself for completing cleaning tasks can make the process more enjoyable and help you stick to your routine. Here are some ideas:

 Small Treats: Indulge in a piece of chocolate, a quick phone game, or an episode of your favorite show after completing a cleaning task.

 Bigger Rewards: Set aside a larger reward, like a relaxing bath or a night out with friends, for completing a bigger cleaning project.

 Celebrate Milestones: Acknowledge your progress, no matter how small. Celebrate with a dance party or a phone call to a loved one.

Tip: Make sure the rewards are genuinely motivating for you. It could be anything that brings you a sense of accomplishment or relaxation.

By using these strategies, you can transform cleaning from a dreaded chore into a series of manageable tasks.

Chapter 5: Conquering Cleaning Consistency: Building Habits that Last

Taming the cleaning beast isn't about a one-time blitz attack; it's about building sustainable habits. This chapter will equip you with strategies to create a cleaning routine that works for your ADHD brain and helps you achieve long-term consistency.

The Power of Routines: Creating a Cleaning Schedule that Sticks

Routines provide structure and predictability, which are essential for ADHD brains. Here's how to create a cleaning schedule that sticks:

Start Small: Don't try to overhaul your entire cleaning routine overnight. Begin with a few manageable tasks and gradually add more as you build consistency.

Schedule Cleaning Sessions: Block out specific times in your calendar for cleaning tasks. Treat these appointments with the same respect you would any other meeting.

Find Your Rhythm: Experiment with daily, weekly, or monthly cleaning schedules depending on your workload and preferences.

Tip: Be realistic about the amount of time a task will take. Don't overload your schedule, or you're setting yourself up for failure.

Habit Stacking: Attach Cleaning to Existing Routines

Our brains form connections between activities. Habit stacking leverages this by attaching a new habit (cleaning) to an existing one (brushing your teeth). Here's how to use it:

Identify Your Routines: Think about your daily and weekly routines, like making coffee in the morning or watching TV at night.

Pair Cleaning with Existing Habits: Add a quick cleaning task before, after, or during your existing routines. For example, wipe down the bathroom counter after brushing your teeth, or fold laundry while watching TV commercials.

Tip: Start with small, easily achievable cleaning tasks to make habit stacking less daunting.

Taming the Perfectionist: Focusing on Progress, Not Perfection

The pursuit of perfection can be a major roadblock to consistency. Here's how to shift your focus to progress:

Celebrate "Good Enough": Accept that "perfect" cleaning might not be realistic or even necessary. Aim for "good enough" and celebrate the progress you've made.

Focus on the Benefits: Remind yourself how much better you feel in a clean and organized space. Let that be your motivation, not the pursuit of flawlessness.

Forgive Yourself for Setbacks: Everyone has setbacks. Don't beat yourself up if you miss a cleaning session. Just get back on track the next day.

Tip: Use positive self-talk. Instead of criticizing yourself for a messy space, say something like, "I can clean this up. I've done it before, and I can do it again."

Enlisting Help (Without Feeling Like a Failure)

Asking for help doesn't mean you're failing. Here are some ways to enlist help:

Involve Family Members: Delegate cleaning tasks to family members based on age and ability.

Hire Help (Even if it's Occasional): Consider hiring a cleaning service for a deep clean or weekly maintenance, depending on your budget.

Swap Cleaning with Friends: Barter cleaning sessions with a friend. You clean their place one week, and they clean yours the next.

Tip: Frame asking for help as a way to create a cleaner, more enjoyable space for everyone, not a sign of weakness.

By using these strategies, you can overcome the challenges of inconsistency and build a cleaning routine that becomes second nature.

Chapter 6: Technology to the Rescue: Apps and Gadgets for ADHD Cleaning

We live in a world of technological marvels, and guess what? Many of them can be your allies in the fight for a clean and organized home. This chapter will explore how to leverage technology to streamline your cleaning routine and make it more manageable with your ADHD brain.

Utilizing Cleaning Timers and Apps

There's an app for (almost) everything, including cleaning! Here are some ways to use apps and timers to your advantage:

Cleaning Timers with Visual Cues: Apps with built-in timers and visual cues, like progress bars or changing colors, can help you stay focused and motivated during cleaning sessions (think of the Pomodoro Technique on steroids!).

To-Do List Apps with Reminders: Utilize apps that allow you to create cleaning to-do lists with customizable reminders to nudge you when it's time to tackle a specific task.

Habit Tracking Apps: Track your cleaning progress on a habit tracker app. Seeing your consistency visually can be incredibly motivating.

Tip: Look for apps with gamified elements or reward systems to make cleaning more fun and engaging.

Smart Home Devices to Automate Tasks (Yes, Really!)

Smart home devices are no longer science fiction. Here's how they can become your cleaning comrades-in-arms:

Robot Vacuums: These little cleaning robots can tackle dust and debris on your floors, freeing up your time and energy for other cleaning tasks.

Smart Thermostats: Program your thermostat to adjust the temperature automatically, reducing dust buildup and creating a more comfortable cleaning environment.

Smart Speakers: Use smart speakers to set cleaning timers, play motivating music, or even control smart lights – all with voice commands, minimizing distractions.

Tip: Consider starting with one or two smart home devices and gradually adding more as you get comfortable with the technology.

Noise-Canceling Headphones: Tuning Out Distractions While You Clean

Background noise can be a major distraction for those with ADHD. Here's how noise-canceling headphones can be your cleaning BFF:

Block Out Distractions: Noise-canceling headphones can help you focus on the cleaning task at hand by blocking out external noise, like barking dogs or loud neighbors.

Immerse Yourself in Motivation: Pair your noise-canceling headphones with upbeat music or podcasts to create a motivating cleaning soundtrack.

Audiobooks and Cleaning: Listen to audiobooks while you clean. It's a great way to keep your mind engaged and prevent boredom during longer cleaning sessions.

Tip: Look for noise-canceling headphones that are comfortable to wear for extended periods, especially if you plan on cleaning for longer stretches.

Investing in Cleaning Tools That Make Life Easier

The right tools can make a world of difference in cleaning efficiency. Here are some investments worth considering:

Lightweight Vacuum Cleaners: For those who struggle with heavy lifting, a lightweight vacuum cleaner can make cleaning floors less physically demanding.

Microfiber Cloths: Microfiber cloths are versatile and effective, reducing the need for multiple cleaning products and minimizing clutter.

Multi-Purpose Cleaning Sprays: Opt for multi-purpose cleaning sprays that can be used on various surfaces to simplify your cleaning routine.

Tip: Research ergonomic cleaning tools that minimize strain on your body, especially if you have any physical limitations.

By embracing technology in these ways, you can transform cleaning from a chore into a more streamlined and efficient process, making it easier to stick to your cleaning routines.

Chapter 7: The One-Minute Tidy: Quick Pick-Me-Ups to Prevent Overwhelm

Maintaining a clean and organized space isn't about achieving a state of perpetual perfection; it's about establishing habits to prevent clutter from accumulating in the first place. This chapter will equip you with strategies for incorporating quick and easy tidying techniques into your daily routine, keeping the chaos at bay and preventing overwhelm.

The "Put-Away Patrol": Training Yourself to Return Items Immediately

One of the biggest contributors to clutter is the "out of sight, out of mind" mentality. Here's how to train yourself to put things away immediately:

The One-Minute Rule: Make a habit of putting away any item you can within a minute of using it. This could be returning a book to the shelf, folding a piece of laundry, or putting dishes in the dishwasher.

Designated Landing Zones: Create temporary landing zones for commonly used items, like a basket for keys and mail near the entryway or a bowl for loose change on a table.

Enlist the Help of Family Members: Turn putting things away into a quick family game or challenge, making it more fun and engaging for everyone.

Tip: Train yourself to notice when something is out of place and take a moment to put it away immediately.

The Evening Reset: A Quick Tidy Before Bed

A few minutes spent tidying before bed can make a world of difference in how you feel the next morning. Here's how to incorporate an evening reset into your routine:

10-Minute Tidy Blitz: Set a timer for 10 minutes and spend that time picking up clutter, putting things away, and wiping down surfaces.
 Focus on High-Traffic Areas: Prioritize tidying high-traffic areas like the kitchen counters, living room tables, and bathroom sink.
 Clear Dishes: Make loading the dishwasher or washing a few dishes part of your evening routine to avoid waking up to a sink full of dirty dishes.

Tip: Put on some relaxing music while you tidy to create a calming pre-bed ritual.

The Weekend Warrior: Scheduling Deeper Cleaning Sessions

Weekly cleaning sessions are essential for maintaining a clean and organized space. Here's how to approach them strategically:

Break Down the Tasks: Divide your cleaning tasks into smaller, more manageable chunks and assign them to specific days of the weekend.
Deep Clean One Area at a Time: Focus on deep cleaning one area of your home each week, like the bathroom on Saturday and the kitchen on Sunday.
Reward Yourself: After completing your weekend cleaning session, reward yourself with a relaxing activity or a fun outing.

Tip: Involve family members in your weekend cleaning sessions to make it a collaborative effort and lighten the load.

By incorporating these quick tidying techniques into your daily and weekly routines, you can prevent clutter from accumulating and maintain a sense of order in your home.

Chapter 8: Embracing Imperfections: Self-Compassion for the ADHD Cleaner

You've learned a multitude of strategies for conquering clutter, creating routines, and leveraging technology to combat cleaning chaos with your ADHD brain. But the journey doesn't end there. This chapter will explore the importance of self-compassion, a powerful tool that will help you navigate setbacks, celebrate progress, and maintain motivation on your cleaning quest.

Letting Go of the "Shoulds": Creating Realistic Expectations

The inner critic loves to bombard us with "shoulds": "I should have cleaned this yesterday," or "My house should be spotless all the time." Here's how to silence the critic and create realistic expectations:

Challenge Negative Thoughts: When you hear a critical thought, challenge it with a more compassionate one. Instead of "I should have cleaned this yesterday," try "It's okay that I didn't clean yesterday. I can do it today."
Set Attainable Goals: Don't try to overhaul your entire cleaning routine overnight. Start with small, achievable goals and gradually build from there.
Focus on Progress, Not Perfection: Celebrate the steps you take forward, no matter how small. Remember, progress, not perfection, is the key to long-term success.

Tip: Reframe cleaning as a form of self-care. A clean and organized space can contribute to a calmer and more positive state of mind.

Forgive Yourself for Setbacks: Progress, Not Perfection

There will be days when cleaning falls by the wayside. Here's how to forgive yourself and get back on track:

Setbacks are Inevitable: Everyone has setbacks. Don't beat yourself up if you miss a cleaning session.

Self-Compassion is Key: Treat yourself with kindness and understanding, just as you would a friend who's struggling.

Pick Yourself Up and Start Again: Don't let a setback derail your progress. Acknowledge it, forgive yourself, and recommit to your cleaning routine.

Tip: Visualize yourself overcoming a cleaning hurdle. Imagine yourself calmly tackling the mess and feeling accomplished afterward.

Celebrating Your Achievements: Building Confidence and Motivation

Taking the time to acknowledge your accomplishments is essential for building confidence and staying motivated. Here's how to celebrate your wins:

Big or Small, Celebrate Them All: Celebrate every milestone, no matter how small. Did you finally conquer that overflowing junk drawer? Treat yourself to a small reward!

Track Your Progress: Keep a visual record of your progress. Take pictures of your organized space or use a habit tracker app to see how far you've come.

Share Your Successes: Share your cleaning victories with loved ones who will support and celebrate your achievements.

Tip: Create a reward system for yourself. Completing a cleaning task could earn you a relaxing bubble bath, a new book, or an evening out with friends.

By embracing self-compassion, you'll develop a more positive and sustainable approach to cleaning. You'll learn to forgive yourself for setbacks, celebrate your progress, and ultimately, find a sense of peace and accomplishment in creating a clean and organized space that works for you and your ADHD brain.

Chapter 9: Long-Term Strategies: Preventing Relapse and Maintaining Order

Congratulations! You've conquered the initial cleaning chaos and established routines that work for you. But the battle against clutter is an ongoing one. This chapter will equip you with long-term strategies to prevent relapse, maintain order, and ensure your cleaning systems continue to serve you well.

Identifying Triggers for Clutter: Understanding Your ADHD Patterns

Understanding what triggers clutter buildup in your home is the first step to preventing it. Here's how to identify your personal clutter culprits:

Emotional Attachment: Do you tend to hold onto things for sentimental reasons, even if they don't serve a purpose?

Impulse Buying: Are you prone to spontaneous purchases that end up adding to the clutter?

Disorganization: Does a lack of designated storage lead to items getting misplaced and forgotten?

By recognizing your triggers, you can develop targeted strategies to address them. For example, if sentimental attachment is a trigger, consider taking photos of items before letting go.

Re-evaluating Regularly: Adapting Systems as Your Needs Change

Our lives and needs are constantly evolving. What worked for you a year ago might not work today. Here's how to ensure your cleaning systems stay relevant:

Schedule Regular Reviews: Set aside time every few months to assess your cleaning routines and storage solutions.

Adapt and Adjust: Don't be afraid to tweak your systems as needed. Maybe you need to declutter a specific category again, or perhaps a new storage solution is necessary.

Embrace Flexibility: Life throws curveballs. Be prepared to adjust your cleaning routines accordingly,   whether it's due to a busy work week or an unexpected illness.

Tip: Involve family members in your re-evaluation process. Their input can be valuable in ensuring the cleaning systems work for everyone in the household.

Creating a Support System: Enlisting Help When Needed

Don't be afraid to ask for help! Here are ways to build a support system for long-term cleaning success:

Involve Family Members: Delegate cleaning tasks or chores to family members based on age and ability.

Hire Help (Even if it's Occasional): Consider hiring a cleaning service for a deep clean or weekly maintenance, depending on your budget.

Support Groups: Connect with online or in-person support groups for people with ADHD. Sharing experiences and tips with others who understand your struggles can be incredibly motivating.

Tip: Frame asking for help as a way to maintain a clean and organized space for everyone, not a sign of weakness.

Remember, creating a clean and organized space is a marathon, not a sprint. By implementing the strategies in this chapter, you'll be well on your way to preventing relapse, maintaining order, and finding a sense of calm and accomplishment in your ADHD-friendly home.

Conclusion: Living with ADHD: Creating Calm and Order in a Chaotic World

Congratulations! You've reached the end of this guide. You've learned a multitude of strategies for tackling clutter, creating cleaning routines, and leveraging technology to combat cleaning chaos with your ADHD brain. But more importantly, you've learned the power of self-compassion – a crucial tool for navigating setbacks, celebrating progress, and maintaining motivation on your journey to a calmer and more organized space.

This guide is just the beginning. Remember, living with ADHD is a unique experience, and the strategies that work for you will evolve over time. Embrace the process, celebrate your victories, and don't be afraid to experiment and find what works best for you. Here are some key takeaways to keep in mind:

Focus on Progress, Not Perfection: Don't get discouraged by setbacks. Celebrate the steps you take forward, no matter how small.

Find Your System: There's no one-size-fits-all approach to cleaning with ADHD. Experiment with different strategies and find what works best for you and your brain.

Embrace Technology: Utilize cleaning apps, timers, and smart home devices to streamline your cleaning routine and make it more manageable.

Self-Compassion is Key: Be kind to yourself. Forgive yourself for setbacks, and acknowledge your accomplishments on your cleaning journey.

With the knowledge and strategies you've gained from this guide, you're well-equipped to create a clean and organized space that works for you and your ADHD brain. This, in turn, can contribute to a calmer, more focused, and overall more positive state of mind. You've got this!

www.ingramcontent.com/pod-product-compliance
Lightning Source LLC
Chambersburg PA
CBHW051702250726
48653CB00007B/2802